A TIME OF WONDER

Daily reflections and prayers for Advent

Siobhán O'Keeffe

kevin mayhew

kevin mayhew

First published in Great Britain in 2012 by Kevin Mayhew Ltd
Buxhall, Stowmarket, Suffolk IP14 3BW
Tel: +44 (0) 1449 737978 Fax: +44 (0) 1449 737834
E-mail: info@kevinmayhewltd.com

www.kevinmayhew.com

ISBN 978 1 84867 529 2
Catalogue No. 1501361

Cover design by Rob Mortonson

Edited by Nicki Copeland
Typeset by Richard Weaver

Printed and bound in Great Britain

Contents

About the author

Siobhán O'Keeffe was born in Cork, Ireland, and is a Sister of the Sacred Hearts of Jesus and Mary (Chigwell Sisters). She is a Registered General Nurse with specialist interest in palliative and dementia care, she offers spirituality and dementia training in Ireland and the UK and works in community outreach programmes in Dagenham, Essex. Siobhán holds an MA in Applied Theology, Justice, Peace and Mission Studies from the Missionary Institute, London. She is the author of two books: *Petals of Prayer – Prayers and Reflections for people with dementia and their carers* and *Beloved of the Lord – Reflections and Resources for people with special needs and their carers*. She enjoys reading, gardening, walking and music appreciation.

For Isabella

Introduction

Advent is a time of adoration of the one who is to come, the Christ of God. We celebrate the divine intervention of God in the person of Jesus Christ. We rejoice that he who is 'Veritas' – the truth – is coming. 'I am the way, and the truth, and the life' (John 14:6). It is a special time of preparation for us so that we may welcome him who is to come.

God bestows his graces upon us so that we are able to turn our hearts and minds to God. We are invited into a special time of repentance, conversion and renewal. It is a season of *trust* and thanksgiving. We entrust our lives to a faithful God who teaches us how to live and who will lead us to the Father who spoke of him on Tabor, 'This is my Son, the Beloved; listen to him!' (Mark 9:7).

Advent is God's gift to us so that we may be drawn into a deepening relationship with the Father. It is a time of joy, hope and expectancy. God wishes to renew our hearts, our churches and our world. He desires that we are deeply in tune with what is really important and sacred in our lives – the presence of the holy.

During this period of grace, we unite ourselves more deeply with him who has called us into being. Infused with his joy we share the good news of him who is with us. We pray that we may all be one in him who is love.

Advent is a time of remembering when God asks us to 'Forget me not'. It is a time of gratitude when we give thanks for what God in his mercy has done for us. God asks us not to forget him:

Do not harden your hearts, as at Meribah,
as on the day at Massah in the wilderness,
when your ancestors tested me,
and put me to the proof, though they had seen
my work.

Psalm 95:8, 9

It is a time of healing and hope, a time when we may lay down our burdens and rest at his feet. 'Come to me, all you that are weary and are carrying heavy burdens, and I will give you rest' (Matthew 11:28). We are invited to ponder with childlike trust the beauty and mystery of the incarnation. A gift is being bestowed upon us that is much greater than anything that is available in the market-place. We are invited to hear God's words of promise to us: 'When you search for me, you will find me; if you seek me with all your heart' (Jeremiah 29:13).

Like Mary, may our pondering on the word of God be the source and root of our lives. 'Mary treasured all these words and pondered them in her heart' (Luke 2:19). May our reminiscence be filled with joy as we give thanks to the one who is to come with a new promise: 'But for you who revere my name the sun of righteousness shall rise, with healing in its wings' (Malachi 4:2).

Advent is a time of forgiveness for all that is not right in our own lives and the life of the world. We are invited, like the prodigal son, to return to the Father and receive his forgiving, healing welcome in our lives. 'His father saw him and was filled with compassion; he ran and put his arms around him and kissed him' (Luke 15:20). We are invited to offer our whole selves to God, that he may indeed be Lord and Master of our lives.

We are invited to offer glory, honour and praise to the eternal God for all that he has offered to us:

I will bless the Lord at all times;
his praise shall continually be in my mouth.
My soul shall make its boast in the Lord.

Psalm 34:1, 2

We are invited to enter ever more deeply into the celebration of the Eucharist. By his coming, God gave himself to us for all eternity and we continue to celebrate his presence with us in the Eucharist.

Our thanksgiving and trust deepen at this time. We entrust an unknown future to a known God. 'For surely I know the plans I have for you, says the Lord, plans for your welfare and not for harm, to give you a future with hope' (Jeremiah 29:11).

We are invited to share in the mission of Jesus during Advent in a special way so that all people may come to know the love of God. It is a time of ministry when we share in the healing, liberating and empowering ministry of Jesus. Like Mary, we are asked to nurture a world that is starving for hope. We are to be other-centred, as Jesus laid down his life for others. It is a season of grace and prayer to deepen our personal and communal adoration of the King who is to come.

First Sunday of Advent

A call to faithfulness

Reading

Mark 13:33-37

Beware, keep alert; for you do not know when the time will come. It is like a man going on a journey, when he leaves home and puts his slaves in charge, each with his work, and commands the doorkeeper to be on the watch. Therefore, keep awake – for you do not know when the master of the house will come, in the evening, or at midnight, or at cockcrow, or at dawn, or else he may find you asleep when he comes suddenly. And what I say to you I say to all: Keep awake.

Reflection

During this time of Advent, we are asked to thank God for all the graces we have received through Jesus. Our lives have been enriched by all the gifts of the Spirit that have been made available to us through Christ (1 Corinthians 12:4-13). We are called to faithfulness; to remain true to the one, true, living God. Gifted by the Holy Spirit, we are asked to live holy and spotless lives in love through the Spirit. God has called us and has joined us to his Son: 'you are not in the flesh; you are in the Spirit, since the Spirit of God dwells in you' (Romans 8:9).

By our baptism, we have been immersed into the heart and life of God; we are now awaiting the new birth of the reconciler, the one who was promised from all eternity in the Scriptures. 'See I am sending my messenger to prepare the way before me, and the Lord whom you seek will suddenly come in his temple. The messenger of the covenant in whom you delight – indeed he is coming, says the Lord of hosts' (Malachi 3:1). In his bountiful mercy, God bestows his Son upon us. 'My soul longs, indeed it faints for the courts of the Lord; my heart and my flesh sing for joy to the living God' (Psalm 84:2).

We may wonder, how do we prepare our hearts for his sacred coming?

Like all the holy people in the Scriptures, we are invited to root our lives in prayer and to seek God in all things:

> So if you have been raised with Christ, seek the things that are above, where Christ is, seated at the right hand of God. Set your minds on things that are above, not on things that are on earth, for you have died, and your life is hidden with Christ in God. When Christ who is your life is revealed, then you also will be revealed with him in glory.
>
> *Colossians 3:1-4*

In the Gospel of Mark, we are asked to stay awake, to be alert to the coming of the Lord. We may ask, how do we do this? We ask God to bestow a gift of deep discernment upon us so that we may recognise him when he comes. We are to be ever alert, ever present to the one who comes in daily visitations to our lives. We meet him in his word, in the sacraments of the church and in our encounters with each other. He is with us in the multitudinous moments of grace that bless our days. Like wise virgins, we fill our lamps with the holy oil of prayer so that we may recognise the Lord when he comes. By his choice of us, we are consecrated and totally given over to the one who is love. We desire to recognise him. In order to do this ever more fully, we ask ourselves:

- What blocks my recognition of him today?
- Is my life changed and transformed by my daily encounters with the living God?
- What is my mission of evangelisation in preparation for the new Advent of the Lord?
- Am I accountable for the gifts and graces that God has bestowed upon me?
- In living well today, I am preparing for my own death. How do I feel about my death and what graces do I need in order to continue to prepare for my death?

God has asked us to be agents of transformation in the world where we live. We are to live by the gospel and not by the values of the world. We are to offer gospel witness to the young and encouragement to the older members of our society. We are asked to be good news people who share the charism of the gospel with every breath that we take. We are an alive, friendly, warm, responsive people who are to be the yeast in the dough and the salt of the earth. We are asked to 'grow in the grace and knowledge of our Lord Jesus Christ' (2 Peter 3:18).

As we celebrate this Advent season, we give thanks for the graces and blessings that God has bestowed upon us since Advent last year.

Jesus wishes to reveal himself in new ways this Advent. We await in a spirit of wonder and praise, expectancy and hope. We turn back to him with all our hearts (Joel 2:12), as he bestows gifts of wisdom and discernment upon us for our world. Like the prophet Daniel, our hearts sing out a song of praise.

Monday

Jesus was amazed!

Reading

Matthew 8:5-11

When he entered Capernaum, a centurion came to him, appealing to him and saying, 'Lord, my servant is lying at home paralysed and in terrible distress.' And he said to him, 'I will come and cure him.' The centurion answered, 'Lord, I am not worthy to have you come under my roof; but only speak the word, and my servant will be healed. For I also am a man under authority, with soldiers under me; and I say to one, "Go", and he goes, and to another, "Come", and he comes, and to my slave, "Do this", and the slave does it.' When Jesus heard him, he was amazed and said to those who followed him, 'Truly I tell you, in no one in Israel have I found such faith.'

Reflection

In this beautiful reading we see the response of Jesus to the pain of the centurion. His servant is ill and he begs Jesus to heal him. The centurion knows who Jesus is and that he has the power to heal the sick. In faith and trust he opens the doors of his home and his heart to the healing power of God. Jesus responds in love to the faith-filled cry of a compassionate employer. He bestows fullness of life upon the sick servant. 'I am going to bring it recovery and healing; I will heal them and reveal to them abundance of prosperity and security' (Jeremiah 33:6).

This is a fitting story for the beginning of Advent. Our merciful God looked on the world and saw that it was in need of healing. The world needed the redemption that could only be offered by the Son of God. God looked with love on the world from all eternity and breathed life upon the earth (Genesis 1–3). God promised, 'But for you who revere my name the sun of righteousness shall rise, with healing in its wings. You shall go out leaping like calves from the stall' (Malachi 4:2) so that the whole world would be transformed and made new. God does not delegate to a lesser being but promises to be with his people in their distress:

> But Moses said to God, 'If I come to the Israelites and say to them, "The God of your ancestors has sent me to you", and they ask me, "What is his name?" what shall I say to them?' God said to Moses, 'I AM WHO I AM.'
>
> *Exodus 3:13, 14*

God has come to rescue all from calamity, destruction and fear. He has heard the cry of the psalmist, 'Answer me when I call, O God of my right! You gave me room when I was in distress. Be gracious to me, and hear my prayer' (Psalm 4:1). God gave his people bread from heaven each day (Exodus 16:4).

During this holy season, God is coming to transform our world into the image of himself. Each new Advent, God offers us an opportunity to be recreated, like the unfinished pot in the potter's house (Jeremiah 18:1-5). Every new baby born is an act of love as God offers us another sign of hope; he has created another person in his image and likeness. His son Jesus is sharing in the Godhead of the Trinity.

During this Advent season we are offered an opportunity to open our hearts in new ways to the healing rays of God's love (Luke 13:12-14). The healing of God is not confined to any nation, class or creed. It is available free of charge to all who dare to say, 'Lord, I am not worthy to have you come under my roof; but only speak the word, and my servant will be healed.'

Prayer

Lord, through the gift of prayer may my
healing,
everlasting,
attentive,
loving,
inviting,
nurturing,
gracious God come to me this day. May he draw me deeper into the mystery and gift of Adam. May he restore and renew me in the depths of my soul. May he burst forth into my life so that, like the centurion, I may dare to ask to receive him into the home of my heart. May his sonship abide within me and draw me deeper into God each day of Advent, each moment of my life.
Amen.

Tuesday

Virtue and beauty are coming

Reading

Luke 10:21-24

At that same hour Jesus rejoiced in the Holy Spirit and said, 'I thank you, Father, Lord of heaven and earth, because you have hidden these things from the wise and the intelligent and have revealed them to infants; yes, Father, for such was your gracious will. All things have been handed over to me by my Father; and no one knows who the Son is except the Father, or who the Father is except the Son and anyone to whom the Son chooses to reveal him.

Reflection

A new dawn will burst upon our world,
the awaited one, the promised one will come;
the sin of Adam will be no more.
Deep within the seed of death
new life lay buried,
now it will come.
Death will be no more.
Integrity, justice and truth will break upon us.

'We will sing of your steadfast love,
O Lord, for ever;
with our mouths we will proclaim
your faithfulness to all generations' (Psalm 89:1, 2, adapted).

Holiness, virtue and beauty are coming;
the degradation of the human spirit will be washed clean;
human trafficking, genocide, nuclear warfare,
the raping of the earth, ethnic cleansing,
neglect of the elderly, child abuse,
all consumed in the fire of his love.
Liberation, compassion, deep inner freedom will be poured out,
the blood of redemption will be poured upon all creation.
Nothing will contain the immensity of his love.

'We wait for new heavens and a new earth,
where righteousness is at home' (2 Peter 3:13).
All will be renewed and made whole;
fear and distrust will fall away in the light of his grace.
Many are chosen to receive this new life,
hand-picked and gifted by the living God,
baptised into his Son.
A new ear will respond,
all hearts will be transformed by the power of his living word;
falling in adoration at the throne of God,
we will offer worship and praise.

Amazing grace is poured upon us as we gaze
upon the face of the living,
omnipotent,
creative,
unifying,
healing God.

Prayer

You invite me, Lord, into the deep room of my heart.
Here you reveal to me who you are;
you bless me with all the blessings of heaven and earth,
you show me your face;
I am made new.
I am gifted and chosen by the living God.
I lay my life open before you.
I give you thanks.
Soaked in your power I step forth
to bring new life to all.
You guide me by new revelations of your love each day,
you lead your people away from the cobra lair of sin;
I join you in the cleansing waters of the Jordan;
in the depths of my heart I hear your life-changing words,
'You are my child in whom I am well pleased.'
I rejoice and am glad.
May eternal glory, honour and praise be yours for evermore.
Amen, Amen, Amen.

Wednesday

The generous self-gift of the virgin

Reading

Matthew 15:29-37

After Jesus had left that place, he passed along the Sea of Galilee, and he went up the mountain, where he sat down. Great crowds came to him, bringing with them the lame, the maimed, the blind, the mute, and many others. They put them at his feet, and he cured them, so that the crowd was amazed when they saw the mute speaking, the maimed whole, the lame walking, and the blind seeing. And they praised the God of Israel.

Then Jesus called his disciples to him and said, 'I have compassion for the crowd, because they have been with me now for three days and have nothing to eat; and I do not want to send them away hungry, for they might faint on the way.' The disciples said to him, 'Where are we to get enough bread in the desert to feed so great a crowd?' Jesus asked them, 'How many loaves have you?' They said 'Seven, and a few small fish.' Then ordering the crowd to sit down on the ground, he took the seven loaves and the fish; and after giving thanks he broke them and gave them to the disciples, and the disciples gave them to the crowds. And all of them ate and were filled; and they took up the broken pieces left over, seven baskets full.

Reflection

In this reflection we meet a God of graciousness who bestows gifts abundantly on his people. God wishes to come to free his people from all burdens. He is attentive to the physical needs of his people and rescues them from all their distress.

Blessings will be bestowed on the people through the generous self-gift of the virgin. She gave all of herself unreservedly so that the kingdom of God could be brought into being. She bore a God who always listens to the cry of the people. All is gift since the time when our transformative God entered our world. He always gave thanks to his Father when he prayed, releasing divine power and energy on all creation. The blind and the deaf were healed, the hungry were fed. Our gracious God takes all that we offer to him and transforms it for the glory of his Father.

As we enter ever more deeply into Advent, our world hungers for the God who is to come. We cry out to the living God as we say, '"The Lord is my portion," says my soul, "therefore I will hope in him"' (Lamentations 3:24).

Today our world is waiting to be rescued from its chaos, like Jonah waiting in the belly of the whale. 'But the Lord provided a large fish to swallow up Jonah; and Jonah was in the belly of the fish for three days and three nights' (Jonah 1:17). Nothing is too ordinary for the attention and loving kindness of the God who is to come. 'Weeping may linger for the night, but joy comes with the morning' (Psalm 30:5). We wait with expectancy and hope for this new revelation of divine love. He will renew the face of the earth.

The new banquet of God's love will be a new and deeper intimacy with himself. He who is to come is a forgiving God who reminds us that 'I will be merciful towards their iniquities, and I will remember their sins no more' (Hebrews 8:12). The mourning veil that has shrouded our world will be removed and a new joy will be born. 'All flesh shall know that I am the Lord your

Saviour, and your Redeemer, the Mighty One of Jacob' (Isaiah 49:26). All idolatry will be washed out of our lives by the blood of the Lamb. Our hearts will continue to learn of the many ways in which he loves us.

We begin our new life in Christ this Advent with a new fire burning in our souls. Like the apostles after the resurrection, 'we cannot keep from speaking about what we have seen and heard' (Acts 4:20). We open the doors of our hearts ever more fully to his love and his desires for our world.

Prayer

During this Advent, I pray in a new way for
all the victims of domestic violence,
all child soldiers,
all who do not have freedom to express their faith, and
all prisoners of conscience.
May the light of a new dawn bring healing and hope
into their lives.
Like a young gazelle, may I run and never tire in my
mission of love.
May my life bear rich fruit for the kingdom of God as
I support all who suffer.
May the light of the gospel shine forth from my eyes;
may it bring healing and hope to all for whom this
Advent signifies a new day.
Amen.

Thursday

A rock foundation

Reading

Matthew 7:24-27

Everyone then who hears these words of mine and acts on them will be like a wise man who built his house on rock. The rain fell, the floods came, and the winds blew and beat on that house, but it did not fall because it had been founded on rock. And everyone who hears these words of mine and does not act on them will be like a foolish man who built his house on sand. The rain fell, and the floods came, and the winds blew and beat against the house, and it fell – and great was its fall!

Reflection

In this reading, we learn of the fate of the unwise builder. He built his house on sand and left it vulnerable to natural disaster. Nothing could save it in the face of a great wind. It rocked, toppled, and fell – and what a fall it was!

This use of imagery reflects our own fate when our lives are rocked with the disaster of sin. The nights of our soul become darkened by forces that threaten us, and all too often we crash to the ground when our weakness and vulnerability consume us.

In our times of struggle, like the psalmist we may cry out to the living God who will reach out and rescue us.

Have mercy on me, O God,
according to your steadfast love;
according to your abundant mercy
blot out my transgressions.
Wash me thoroughly from my iniquity,
and cleanse me from my sin.

Psalm 51:1, 2

Today, our world and the Church are victims of many falls: revelations of abuse, corruption, lack of faith, and so on. During this Advent, our God wishes to step into this abyss and rescue us. In the core of our souls we realise, like the disciples, that there is no other place to which we can turn and receive new life. We desire to go to God, as he has promised us that he has come 'that they may have life, and have it abundantly' (John 10:10).

Our merciful God looks upon us with eyes of great love and draws us to himself. We may be stripped bare by our sin but he allows our experience of nothingness to be used to draw us to himself. Open to his grace, we are drawn deeper into God. He who is to come was stripped of everything so that he could go ever deeper into the Godhead and bless the world with redemption. This is the world that our God wishes us to share, hence he comes among us in new ways each Advent.

Today, our God wishes to draw us to himself through our daily commitment to him in our lives. Our fidelity to our vocations as single people, married people, priests or as consecrated religious is our way to the Father. We echo the prayer of the holy ones of old: 'I will pay my vows to the Lord in the presence of all his people' (Psalm 116:14). We ask for the grace to surrender our wills to him so that his will be done in us – 'not my will but yours be done' (Luke 22:42) – and that God may be praised. We give thanks to the one who is to overcome the power of sin and death by obeying the will of the Father. 'But thanks be to God, who gives us the victory through our Lord Jesus Christ' (1 Corinthians 15:57). We need to have an honest dependency on the grace of God so that, like Jesus, we may know and do the will of the Father.

At times we may echo the prayer of St Paul:

> I can will what is right, but I cannot do it. For I do not do the good I want, but the evil I do not want is what I do. Now if I do what I do not want, it is no longer I that do it, but sin that dwells within me.
>
> *Romans 7:18-20*

Advent is a time of grace, a time when honest confession of our sin allows us to fall into the arms of a merciful God. Our relationship with the living God will be restored and we will be made whole.

Like St Paul, we may ask ourselves if we desire conversion. If we do, we will build our lives on a rock of prayer as the sea of redemption comes to wash all our sins away. Following our personal and communal conversion we are called to be builders of God's kingdom on earth. We will be light bearers directing the people to the star born in Bethlehem.

Prayer

At this time of Advent, I pray in a special way for all who are victims of flooding – the people of Bangladesh, Thailand, victims of tsunami.

I pray also for those who live on natural fault lines and suffer earthquakes and other disasters.

I pray for people who work in mines. I pray for all who have lost loved ones in the mines.
I pray for the grace to hear God's call to conversion this Advent. May the scales fall from my eyes and heart, just as they did for St Paul. May I praise the living God.
Amen.

Friday

What do you desire?

Reading

Matthew 9:27-31

As Jesus went on from there, two blind men followed him, crying loudly, 'Have mercy on us, Son of David!' When he entered the house, the blind men came to him; and Jesus said to them, 'Do you believe that I am able to do this?' They said to him, 'Yes, Lord.' Then he touched their eyes and said, 'According to your faith let it be done to you.' And their eyes were opened. Then Jesus sternly ordered them, 'See that no one knows of this.' But they went away and spread the news about him throughout that district.

Reflection

During this Advent season, our God is coming to bless all the people of God with new sight. We will enter into the rays of his glory so that we may worship him. Our God wishes to heal any spiritual or emotional blindness that mars our lives at this time. In gentleness and humility he asks us, 'What do you desire of me? What can I do for you?' In love he reaches out to touch us and make us whole. We will look on him with new sight. We will be drawn deeper into the mystery of who he is.

Our God of compassion wishes to touch the most intimate personal details of who we are and renew us in ever new ways. He promises to journey with us through all the seasons of our lives and to be the light for our paths.

Ever grateful for his loving invitation, we enter into a deepening relationship with him.

We name for him and for ourselves all that blocks this relationship of intimacy and lay it before him. Fully aware of who we are, he knows everything about us, but confession of our creaturehood deepens our trust in him and our bond of friendship with our incarnate God. The more we reveal to him, the more fully he can heal us. Like the man born blind, our sight can be restored (John 9:1-25).

During this time of Advent, we remember that a God of hope is coming to us. He wishes us to be rooted and grounded in hope. Our lives will be secure in a new way. We will always look to him to be the guide and light of our lives.

Embedded in the hope of Christ, our world will be immersed in the peace that only the God of salvation can offer. Our hearts will open more widely to all the people of the world. His presence is what we desire as we wait with expectant faith for him who is to come.

Joy will burst forth from our souls. We will be unable to contain this joy. We will wish to share everything that he has done for us as we look on him who has loved us so deeply that he chose to come among us. We will wish to share with all whom we meet the vision of our God that he has bestowed upon us. Glory be to him forever. Amen.

Prayer

I pray for all who are blind. I pray that medical research will continue to find a cure for different diseases of the eyes.

I pray for all who care for the blind. Guide and bless them in their work.

I pray that my spiritual blindness may be healed. During this holy season of Advent, may I open my heart more fully to the healing rays of the eternal God who is coming among us.
Amen.

Saturday

A sacred mission

Reading

Matthew 9:35-38

Then Jesus went about all the cities and villages, teaching in their synagogues, and proclaiming the good news of the kingdom, and curing every disease and every sickness. When he saw the crowds, he had compassion for them, because they were harassed and helpless, like sheep without a shepherd. Then he said to the disciples, 'The harvest is plentiful, but the labourers are few; therefore ask the Lord of the harvest to send out labourers into his harvest.'

Reflection

During this holy season our hearts rejoice. Our gracious, merciful, generous God is coming to dwell among us. In his benevolence he will bless our world in new ways. Our world will be transformed by the graciousness of his presence. Our hearts rejoice and give thanks. We welcome you, O God.

God has promised us that the reign of God is going to overshadow us. He wishes us to share in his mission of salvation. Gifted and chosen by the Holy Spirit, we are to be partakers in this sacred mission of sharing the good news of the reign of God. Our world is starving for a message of hope – a message that God is asking us to share.

Everything has been gifted to us free of charge. We are asked and obliged to share his living word with all the people of God. God wishes that all may know the joy of their hearts burning within them as he talks to them on the road and opens the Scriptures for them, just as it was for the disciples (Luke 24:32).

Jesus has returned to his Father and entrusted this sacred mission to us. We open our hearts to receive him this Advent so that he may make his home within us. Our hearts are full of joy. We wish to share the joy of his coming with one and all.

Prayer

Fill me, Lord, with your Spirit, that I may know what hope your call holds for me. 'Let us hold fast to the confession of our hope without wavering, for he who has promised is faithful' (Hebrews 10:23).
May I be an ambassador for you, O God (2 Corinthians 5:20). May I be a generous partaker in your mission of love to all. I make this prayer to you, O generous, benevolent, compassionate God. May I welcome your message very eagerly and may many believe (Acts 17:11, 12).
Amen.

Questions for reflection

- What are the arms that I need to lay down this Advent?
- Am I a participant in any form of neglect or abuse?
- Do I turn a deaf ear to the cry of the poor?
- Do I wish to be born into the life of the one who is to come?
- What is the prayer of thanks that I wish to offer to God today?

Questions for reflection and discussion

- Do we dare to ask God to come into our worlds today? The worlds of our hearts, of our local and church communities, of our global environment?
- Are we indifferent to his presence or our need of him?
- Are we like the people of Meribah whose hearts have grown cold?
- Are we consumed by distractions, overwhelmed by the pain of broken relationships or submerged in all forms of crisis?

Second Sunday of Advent

Pray for the peace of Jerusalem

Reading

Mark 1:1-8

The beginning of the good news of Jesus Christ, the Son of God. As it is written in the prophet Isaiah, 'See, I am sending my messenger ahead of you, who will prepare your way; the voice of one crying in the wilderness: "Prepare the way of the Lord, make his paths straight"'. John the baptiser appeared in the wilderness, proclaiming a baptism of repentance for the forgiveness of sins. And people from the whole Judean countryside and all the people of Jerusalem were going out to him, and were baptised by him in the river Jordan, confessing their sins. Now John was clothed with camel's hair, with a leather belt around his waist, and he ate locusts and wild honey. He proclaimed, 'The one who is more powerful than I is coming after me; I am not worthy to stoop down and untie the thong of his sandals. I have baptised you with water; but he will baptise you with the Holy Spirit.'

Reflection

During this time we are invited to pray for the peace of Jerusalem. We are reassured that the one who is to come will bring peace. The God of all consolation is coming to live among us. Our hope rests on this promise. This hope is not deceptive because the Spirit we received in baptism rests deep in our hearts. This spirit reaches out to greet and welcome the God who is to come.

We are reminded of the words of Elizabeth: 'For as soon as I heard the sound of your greeting, the child in my womb leapt for joy' (Luke 1:44). Our spirits, too, leap for joy in the knowledge that the Prince of Peace wishes to live with us.

He wishes to offer us the consolation of his Spirit in the daily realities of our lives. He desires to enter the mystery of each day and bless it with his peace. The jagged edges of our lives, the valleys of suffering and the mountains of despair that attempt to swallow us up will conform with his will of peace for us. All heartache will melt away before the gaze of his love. As we sit still in his presence or reach out to care for his people, the gentle voice of his Spirit will move deep within our souls. We will respond to his call to live holy, spotless and just lives so that we may recognise him when he comes.

We will work with him for the restoration of humanity to all its fullness (John 10:10). We will challenge all forms of injustice and work for the building of the new Jerusalem here on earth. We will reveal to him the arms race and power struggles that plague our hearts and destroy our peace. We will bow down in surrender and loving gratitude to the God of all consolation. We will unite with him in the preparation of the soil of our lives so that his kingdom may come, his will may be done and his reign may overshadow all our lives. United as one body, we the blessed and chosen will sing out his praise on the most holy night. We will undo our sandals because the place where he rests is the most holy ground. We wish to worship him.

Prayer

I ask, Lord, for the grace to live a holy life as I await the coming of the Lord.
May my life be lived in simplicity and truth.
May my heart be free of the baggage and weight of sin.
May I be single-minded in my search for the truth.
May I desire to be truly a child of the Lamb.
May all nations work together for peace in the Middle East.
May the reign of the God of all consolation flood the earth with peace.
May all bow down to undo the sandals of the Lord of peace.
Amen.

Monday

Friend, your sins are forgiven you

Reading

Luke 5:17-26

One day, while he was teaching, Pharisees and teachers of the law were sitting nearby (they had come from every village of Galilee and Judea and from Jerusalem); and the power of the Lord was with him to heal. Just then some men came, carrying a paralysed man on a bed. They were trying to bring him in and lay him before Jesus; but finding no way to bring him in because of the crowd, they went up on the roof and let him down with his bed through the tiles into the middle of the crowd in front of Jesus. When he saw their faith, he said, 'Friend, your sins are forgiven you.' Then the scribes and the Pharisees began to question, 'Who is this who is speaking blasphemies? Who can forgive sins but God alone?' When Jesus perceived their questionings, he answered them, 'Why do you raise such questions in your hearts? Which is easier, to say, "Your sins are forgiven you", or to say, "Stand up and walk"? But so that you may know that the Son of Man has authority on earth to forgive sins' – he said to the one who was paralysed – 'I say to you, stand up and take your bed and go to your home.' Immediately he stood up before them, took what he had been lying on, and went to his home, glorifying God. Amazement seized all of them, and they glorified God and were filled with awe, saying, 'We have seen strange things today.'

Reflection

Lo, your king comes to you;
triumphant and victorious is he,
humble and riding on a donkey,
on a colt, the foal of a donkey.

Zechariah 9:9

This is God's promise to us each day of this Advent season. He reminds us of his faithful love as we await the splendour of our God amongst us.

He wishes to breathe life into our inner cities, slum dwellings and shanty towns. He will come to the areas that are ridden with debt, social unrest and despair. He wishes to reach out in compassion to the long-term unemployed who wish to work and fear that they may never do so again. He will go to the margins where nobody goes and touch pimps, prostitutes and drug dealers with his redeeming presence. 'Black spots' of vice will be no more when he walks amongst all who have chosen another path. He will ask all who are involved in modern-day slave trafficking to turn back to him and 'let my people go, so that they may worship me' (Exodus 8:20). He will touch the 'mats' of unforgiveness, revenge, jealousy and hatred on which we lie and call us back to life.

He will pour his grace on all so that 'if anyone strikes you on the right cheek, turn the other also' may be the motto they follow (Matthew 5:39). He will ask that we 'put [our] sword back into its place; for all who take the sword will perish by the sword' (Matthew 26:52). He will offer a special invitation to all who are tempted to take some water and wash their hands (Matthew 27:24) to draw closer to his forgiving heart.

He will call to conversion all who abuse the elderly or ignore the gifts of people with special educational needs.

A word of challenge will go forth from his mouth to all who promote policies of globalisation as the place on which we are standing is 'holy ground' (Exodus 3:5), not 'a market-place' (John 2:16). The message of good news that he will bring will be, 'Truly I tell you, just as you did it to one of the least of these who are members of my family, you did it to me' (Matthew 25:40).

Prayer

Lord, may I 'rise before the aged, and defer to the old; and may I fear my God. May I know you as the Lord' (Leviticus 19:32, adapted). May I and all your people rejoice because you will come and save us (Isaiah 35:4). Amen.

Tuesday

You call us home

Reading

Matthew 18:12-14

What do you think? If a shepherd has a hundred sheep, and one of them has gone astray, does he not leave the ninety-nine on the mountains and go in search of the one that went astray? And if he finds it, truly I tell you, he rejoices over it more than over the ninety-nine that never went astray. So it is not the will of your Father in heaven that one of these little ones should be lost.

Reflection

Today our prayer is a prayer of thanks. This is a wonderful time to stop, reflect and give thanks for all that God has done for us. He is true to his promises and so often we have been overwhelmed by his generosity and goodness to us. However, so often, like the lepers whom he cured, we fail to thank him (Luke 17:16-18). It is important that we express our sorrow for this hardness of heart. We have not always listened to his voice but he still says, 'Return to the Lord, your God, for he is gracious and merciful' (Joel 2:13). He does not wish that anyone be lost and he will keep seeking us until we are able to return to him. Like the prodigal father, he keeps looking out for us. He waits with expectancy and hope until our shadow falls on the path before him (Luke 15:11-32).

We are to remember to thank God for the many times he has reached out to rescue us from the lonely hillsides on which we lay. We have wandered far from home and far from him. We have not even recognised that we are caught in the brambles of sin or despair, but he casts his healing light into the deepest parts of our hearts. He calls us home.

When we are weak, broken and starved, he touches us with a word of comfort and reminds us that he does not wish us to be lost but desires that we find our home in him. He desires that we listen to his voice and follow him (John 10:27). He invites us to abandon ourselves to his embrace and rest in his arms. He wants us to feel secure in his love and not to struggle against him. So often we are tempted to fight against him. We may fear what he may ask of us, but the bottom line is that we do not trust him enough. So often we do not trust ourselves, but he still seeks us out and calls us home.

Prayer

I thank you, O Lord, that I can 'sing aloud of your steadfast love in the morning. For you have been a fortress for me and a refuge on the day of my distress' (Psalm 59:16). May I listen to your voice of love, walk in your way and always feel that I can return to you, O God of Advent. Amen.

Wednesday

Lost in tinsel

Reading

Matthew 11:28-30

Come to me, all you that are weary and are carrying heavy burdens, and I will give you rest. Take my yoke upon you, and learn from me; for I am gentle and humble in heart, and you will find rest for your souls. For my yoke is easy and my burden is light.

Reflection

Today, the Lord invites us to come to him. He sees with his all-seeing eyes that we are caught up in frenetic activity during this holy season. He witnesses us traipsing through the shops, weighed down with parcels and baggage of every kind. He looks into our hearts and sees that we are pulled away from prayer and that we get lost in tinsel and wrapping of every kind. Our purses are becoming lighter and our hearts heavier. We have lost our way in a culture that is dominated with consumer values, and we are not at peace.

God invites us into a place of silence so that we may hear his voice. In the stillness he reminds us that this is indeed a holy season dedicated to him. He asks us to make our home in him, and we know that when we do our hearts will be deeply at peace. This is not a peace that a consumer world can offer, but one that is a generous gift to us from the God who is love.

Our desire is that the Lord be the centre of our lives and we ask him for the grace to set aside a period of quiet each day to hear his gentle, healing voice. Filled with his Spirit we will step out into the world to share the good news of his great love for all.

Prayer

Lord, I ask for the grace to be faithful to a time of quality prayer every day of my life. May the fullness of life you bestow on me reveal your goodness to all your people. May I know the joy of knowing you as the Lord and centre of my life. I will praise you eternally, O God of all life.
Amen.

Thursday

Living water

Reading

Isaiah 41:13

I, the Lord your God,
hold your right hand;
it is I who say to you, 'Do not fear,
I will help you.'

Reflection

These are words of reassuring promise from God. God in Christ will help us in every situation. This is the meaning of the promise of Advent.

Our God is coming and he will enter into all the details of our lives and transform them. God is a God of redemption, a God of blessing. He is coming anew like the dawn and he will respond like he did of old to the realities of the day. His response will be appropriate for this moment in history.

In ages past, God promised a redeemer to his people:

> The Lord swore to David a sure oath
> from which he will not turn back:
> 'One of the sons of your body
> I will set on your throne.'
>
> *Psalm 132:11*

God is ever faithful to his promises.

In many parts of the world today, people still thirst for water and there is none. This may be due to poor rainfall, inadequate drainage or irrigation systems that have broken down. All too often, people die or suffer grievously from water-borne diseases as they thirst for life-giving, refreshing water. The media abounds with stories of typhoons, floods and other natural disasters that deprive people of the basic human necessity that is water.

Deeper than any ocean is our spiritual thirst for the living water of the gospel. We thirst for the incarnate, redeeming Son of God. His life flows through us and seeps into our souls if we immerse ourselves in the healing springs of his love. The silence of prayer is the oasis in which this spring of living water can well up and refresh the soil of our souls and the fibres of our human spirits. Washed clean by this new life, we are able to move out in loving service to those who thirst for the living God.

We wish to challenge unjust structures that deprive the poor of human rights in their finest details. One such right is the availability of sufficient clean water for all the needs of people, livestock and crops. We pray for and work with government and social policymakers to ensure that good infrastructures for humanitarian aid are put in place in the poorest countries. We cry out for accountability with regard to resource allocation and for a timely response to natural disasters. As committed Christians we strive to work for life-giving policies for the preservation of the environment. We cry out:

> The Lord is good to all,
> and his compassion is over all that he has made.
>
> *Psalm 145:9*

We know that we are called to rise up and be the voice of the voiceless in these realities of our day. Yes, our God who is coming is a compassionate God, but he asks us who have been chosen to be co-heirs with Christ to share in his healing, liberating and empowering mission to all who thirst in the twenty-first century.

Prayer

Grace me, O Living Water, with a deep desire to be transformed in the core of my soul.
Fill me with the water of your Spirit, that I may work for the freedom of all who suffer. Cleanse our world of its indifference to the poor.
Forgive me for my lack of respect for the environment, especially your life-giving water. Through the power of my baptism may I be an agent of change in the society in which I live.
As one voice, may all your people cry out, 'All your works shall give thanks to you, O Lord, and all your faithful shall bless you' (Psalm:145:10).
I praise you, O Living Water.
Amen.

Friday

The joy of listening

Reading

Isaiah 48:17-19

Thus says the Lord,
your Redeemer, the Holy One of Israel:
I am the Lord your God,
who teaches you for your own good,
who leads you in the way you should go.
O that you had paid attention to my commandments!
Then your prosperity would have been like a river,
and your success like the waves of the sea;
your offspring would have been like the sand,
and your descendants like its grains;
their name would never have been cut off or destroyed from before me.

Reflection

In this reading we are reminded that our joy and peace rest in listening attentively to the voice of God in our daily lives. During this Advent, we recommit ourselves to listen to the call of God's commandments and to respond in love to each one. Each commandment is a signpost for our relationship with God and others.

Our Redeemer, the Holy One of Israel, promises us that when we live by the commandments that are laid down by him, our lives will be richly blessed. Fruitfulness in all its many guises will be ours. The happiness that we seek will burst forth from our souls. Like the psalmist we will ponder on the words of our God through the day and long into the night. Our hunger for him who is to come will be insatiable. Nothing less than the living God will satisfy the deep desire that he has placed within us, and we will bear light for the world. This is a ray of the light that is his gift to us.

In times past, people used different signs and omens to find their way to a destination. The wise men followed a star and found the Christ child in a stable.

In the book of Exodus, we read that Moses received the commandments of God on Mount Sinai. Each commandment is a star to guide us in our relationship with God and with each other. Each commandment is interlinked with every other commandment, and each is based on the great law of love: 'Love the Lord your God with all your heart, and with all your soul, and with all your strength, and with all your mind; and your neighbour as yourself' (Luke 10:27).

In our humanity we struggle to live out the commandments in our daily lives. We each have our own areas of weakness. At times, the weight of our sin or fragility can leave us feeling crushed or disheartened. We wonder if we will ever grow in our spiritual lives or be the people God desires us to be. Like the Apostle Paul, we each have our own 'thorn in the flesh' (2 Corinthians 12:7), our Achilles heel, that can negatively impact our relationships with those closest to us. So often we feel ashamed, but we are reminded that 'My grace is sufficient for you, for power is made perfect in weakness' (2 Corinthians 12:8).

In the mystery and beauty of Advent, God reminds us that he wishes to come to us and fill us with fresh hope in his presence with us. He will be the light that will guide us to the Father if we will listen to him.

> O that today you would listen to his voice!
> Harden not your hearts, as at Meribah.
>
> *Psalm 95:7, 8*

He is the God who wishes to banish all violence from our hearts and from our world. He will bring peace. If peace is to reign, our individual and communal lives need to bow down before the living, redeeming God.

In the stillness, we receive grace for our lives to be transformed. Each transformed life builds up the kingdom of God. A peace that is the fruit of justice is born. Our God lives amongst us in our fragile hearts and wounded world.

Prayer

Grace me, O God, with a new and fresh desire to come to you in my nothingness this Advent.
May I live by the Spirit and be guided by the Spirit (Galatians 5:25).
May I become conscious of the areas of the commandments that I ignore, avoid or feel unable to follow.
Melt my fear of retribution by your gaze of love.
I know, Lord, that you are a compassionate and forgiving God.
You ask me to be honest with myself and with you so that you can strengthen and heal me.
I desire to follow you as you would wish me to.
I wish to walk in your ways and to be guided by the star that leads to God.
Amen.

Saturday

That we may see

Reading

Matthew 17:10-13

And the disciples asked him, 'Why, then, do the scribes say that Elijah must come first?' He replied, 'Elijah is indeed coming and will restore all things; but I tell you that Elijah has already come, and they did not recognise him, but they did to him whatever they pleased. So also the Son of Man is about to suffer at their hands.'

Reflection

This passage of Scripture is well placed at this time of Advent. We have travelled a faith journey and are now being challenged to believe more deeply in the one who is to come. We ask ourselves, do we really believe that Jesus is coming, and if so, what difference will his birth make in our lives? How will we receive him? Do we truly believe that his birth has the power to transform our world into a better place for all at this time in the twenty-first century?

History reminds us of the fate of many of the prophets of old. Like Elijah, they suffered greatly at the hands of those to whom they were sent. Matthew reminds us that this will also be the fate of 'the Son of Man'. Is this the pattern we wish to embrace?

Each new Advent is a wonderful opportunity for each of us to choose how we will receive the Son of Man into our lives. The quality of our interpersonal relationships, our response to the poor and the way we care for creation determine how we will welcome the Son of Man. A failure to love in any area of our lives casts a shadow over our relationships with God and with others.

Prayer

This is a time of new awakening for me. I ask for the grace to receive the Son of Man with my heart and mind renewed. May my life be transformed and may society be made whole by his presence amongst us.
Amen.

Questions for reflection and discussion

- How accountable are you and your family or community for the use of water in your homes?
- What do you need to do to reflect your Christian faith in this area of your life?
- What national and local government water policies need to be addressed at this time?

Third Sunday of Advent

Rejoicing Sunday

Reading

Luke 5:1-11

Once while Jesus was standing beside the lake of Gennesaret, and the crowd was pressing in on him to hear the word of God, he saw two boats there at the shore of the lake; the fishermen had gone out of them and were washing their nets. He got into one of the boats, the one belonging to Simon, and asked him to put out a little way from the shore. Then he sat down and taught the crowds from the boat. When he had finished speaking, he said to Simon, 'Put out into the deep water and let down your nets for a catch.' Simon answered, 'Master, we have worked all night long but have caught nothing. Yet if you say so, I will let down the nets.' When they had done this, they caught so many fish that their nets were beginning to break. So they signalled to their partners in the other boat to come and help them. And they came and filled both boats, so that they began to sink. But when Simon Peter saw it, he fell down at Jesus' knees, saying, 'Go away from me, Lord, for I am a sinful man!' For he and all who were with him were amazed at the catch of fish that they had taken; and so also were James and John, sons of Zebedee, who were partners with Simon. Then Jesus said to Simon, 'Do not be afraid; from now on you will be catching people.' When they had brought their boats to shore, they left everything and followed him.

Reflection

At this time of Advent, we are drawing closer to the coming of the Son of God. We are invited into a deeper repentance as the kingdom of God is close at hand. Our repentance is enriched with the knowledge that the good news is being offered to us. This life-giving gift is in direct contrast to the death-dealing journey of sin.

The good news is a message to be shared with all people. Jesus invited Simon and Andrew into a special relationship with him so that they would know him more deeply and learn from him who was meek and humble of heart. Infused with joy, they left everything and followed Jesus.

Jesus had not yet completed his mission of invitation. The fishermen James and John were amongst the elect of God and chosen by Jesus to follow him. They did so without reserve, leaving all to follow their Lord and Master.

We, too, are the elect of God and gifted with a belief in the one who is to come. Advent offers us an opportunity for our faith to grow deeper and our love more pure. Infused with joy, we are asked to share in the work of evangelisation and invite others to learn about the good news of the kingdom of God. To do so, we need to leave everything that does not draw us to God and follow with undivided hearts him who is love. We, too, will learn from him. The joy, hope and witness of our lives will draw others to God. We may never have to use words.

Prayer

Lord, I thank you for your invitation to me to draw closer to you during this holy season. Through the power of your Holy Spirit, may you enlighten me to the things in my life that draw me away from you. May I

repent with true sorrow and live in the light of your law. May I be a beacon of hope to all. May your people know the joy of salvation afresh this Advent. I make this prayer in your name, O God who is to come.
Amen.

Monday

God saw that it was good

Reading

Genesis 1:11, 12

Then God said, 'Let the earth put forth vegetation: plants yielding seed, and fruit trees of every kind on earth that bear fruit with the seed in it.' And it was so. The earth brought forth vegetation: plants yielding seed of every kind, and trees of every kind bearing fruit with the seed in it. And God saw that it was good.

Reflection

At this time of Advent, we bless, praise and adore the Lord our God for the beauty and wonder of his creation. From the dawn of creation, all was his free gift to us. His Spirit has continued to hover over our earth, calling forth life in all its wonder and beauty.

In his coming this Advent, we ask the Lord once again to cleanse our earth of all that is not of him. His creation in all its fullness, diversity and richness is his gift to us and we are his modern-day stewards. We wish to honour the trust that he has placed in us as 'it is required of stewards that they should be found trustworthy' (1 Corinthians 4:2).

Yet God's heart weeps when he witnesses the pillage of the earth when it is used for the cultivation of death-dealing drugs and other toxic substances. People are robbed of their human dignity, and the life that is his gift is snuffed out at the hands of unscrupulous, financially motivated, lawbreaking drug dealers. The cultivation and distribution of illegal drugs is endemic across the world today and contravenes his great law of love. His words 'You shall not murder' (Deuteronomy 5:17) have fallen on poor soil, and anguish and heartbreak are the legacy borne by families until the end of their lives. True to the nature of God, he wishes to offer an alternative message to our world – one of hope and direction to society:

> Maintain justice, and do what is right,
> for soon my salvation will come,
> and my deliverance be revealed.
>
> *Isaiah 56:1*

Prayer

I thank you, O God, for this message of love. I ask that I may walk in your truth and share a message of your salvation with all your people at this time. I pray that our governments and social policymakers write and implement appropriate policies that respond to this pillage of the earth and degradation of human life. May this suffering be washed out by the blood of the Lamb who is to come.
Amen.

Tuesday

The breath of God

Reading

Psalm 103:1, 2

Bless the Lord, O my soul,
and all that is within me,
bless his holy name.
Bless the Lord, O my soul,
and do not forget all his benefits.

Reflection

On this holy day of Advent, we take a little time to reflect over the past year. We wish to acknowledge the many ways in which God has blessed us this year. Every breath that we have inhaled and exhaled has been a free gift from God to us. God's life-giving breath has sustained us in our natural life. Equally, the Spirit of God has hovered over us so that we may be strengthened in our inner being with power through his Spirit (Ephesians 3:16) and remain alive in his love.

During this year we have all lived through our own moments of dying and rising. Our spirits may have rejoiced deeply and wept bitterly as we have trod at times what may have been anguish-laden paths. Somehow, in the midst of it all, our God who comes has shared our journey and we wish to thank him.

Through the power and grace of this most holy season of Advent, we invoke the Holy Spirit whom we received at baptism to fill us with a new and fresh awareness of God's graciousness to us through each moment of our lives. All too often, we forget to savour God's goodness to us and to give thanks.

May we all share in the 'in-breath and out-breath of God' this Advent. May we welcome our newborn king with a spirit of gratitude and may we rejoice deeply.

We give thanks that the long night of sin is ending and the light of a new dawn is breaking upon us.

Prayer

As I prepare for his birth into new life, may I once more prepare my heart in a spirit of humility and praise. May I be washed clean of all indifference and fear. May I truly rejoice in the 'in-breath and out-breath of God', this Advent and always.
Amen.

Wednesday

Beloved of the Lord

Reading

1 Corinthians 1:4-9

I give thanks to my God always for you because of the grace of God that has been given you in Christ Jesus, for in every way you have been enriched in him, in speech and knowledge of every kind – just as the testimony of Christ has been strengthened among you – so that you are not lacking in any spiritual gift as you wait for the revealing of our Lord Jesus Christ. He will also strengthen you to the end, so that you may be blameless on the day of our Lord Jesus Christ. God is faithful; by him you were called into the fellowship of his Son, Jesus Christ our Lord.

Reflection

On this day of Advent our hearts rejoice. We are invited deeper into the mystery of the incarnation. God is pouring his Holy Spirit afresh upon us so that we can be consumed by the fire of his divine love. God is reaching down into the deepest core of our lives and is drawing us ever deeper to himself. All this is a free gift to us, so great is his love for us. We are the people of the Lamb, the chosen, beloved of the Lord. Our hearts rejoice.

Our God is calling us and he is faithful. True to his word, he reminds us once more that it is he who will keep us faithful to himself to the end. In his great love for us, he wishes us to share in his divine life. This is the greatest gift we could ever desire and it is free to us, his beloved.

Our gentle God reminds us that we can look forward with expectant hearts to his coming amongst us. We have no need to fear. Invited into this deep relationship with him, we wish to live holy and spotless lives before the divine Son of God. We have never known a joy so deep, a promise so great. We rejoice and give thanks to the God who in love invites us to share the life of his only begotten Son. This indeed is the message of Advent.

Prayer

I give you thanks, O God, that I am a chosen one, a child of the new Jerusalem. I rejoice and give thanks. May my life bear living witness to this great truth of your love. Amen.

Thursday

Throw open the door of your heart

Reading

Luke 23:34

Father, forgive them; for they do not know what they are doing.

Reflection

This may seem like an unusual prayer for Advent. We usually echo this prayer when we reflect on the sufferings of Christ in his Passion. It is indeed a Holy Week prayer, but it is also an appropriate prayer on which to ponder when we think of the sin of the world at this time. Today, let us share it in the light of our own and the world's resistance to his coming more deeply into our lives.

During Advent, we hear many calls to conversion. The message of the Scriptures invites us to 'prepare the way of the Lord, make his paths straight' (Mark 1:3). However, sadly, we have not always lived by the grace of the Holy Spirit and guarded 'the good treasure' that has been entrusted to us (2 Timothy 1:14). We have given way to 'the sin that clings so closely' (Hebrews 12:1). We have walked in paths that do not lead us deeper into God. Through the power of the Holy Spirit we become conscious of some areas of our own vulnerability. We are also aware that those who share our community life with us or work beside us know our weaknesses. At times, we do not take the message of the gospel to heart but walk in the ways of a secular world. We bow down before false gods and do not listen with the ear of our hearts to the cry of the poor. There is little or no room in the inns of our hearts for the living God.

This holy space can be cluttered with losses, griefs, resentments, struggles and workplace projects and concerns. All can serve to draw us away from our centre wherein lives the living God. There are wounds and heartaches that only his coming can penetrate and heal.

On occasion, the consumerism of the high street draws people away from the true meaning of Advent and Christmas. The allures of our hearts that lead us away from God go deeper than last-minute shopping bargains and need a deeper anointing of his grace so that we may be freed from all that is not of God in our lives.

Fortunately, through the power of baptism and the anointing oil of forgiveness, God renews our hope. 'In his name the Gentiles will hope' (Matthew 12:21). Through the power of his grace, we are able to throw open the door of our hearts and invite him into all the rooms of the inns of our inner beings. His healing rays set us free and we rejoice in his love. We offer him the gift of ourselves as he has loved us first. God as our creator desires all of our being. He wishes that we praise him with every fibre of our souls. When we live in this way,

> neither death, nor life, nor angels, nor rulers, nor things present, nor things to come, nor powers, nor height, nor depth, nor anything else in all creation, will be able to separate us from the love of God in Christ Jesus our Lord.
>
> *Romans 8:38*

Prayer

At this time of Advent, may I rest in the swaddling clothes of his grace. May I know a peace born of his mercy. May I cry out with all the holy ones, 'praise, glory and honour be yours, divine Son of God.'
Amen, Amen, Amen.

Friday

The cry of the elderly

Reading

Isaiah 40:3-5

A voice cries out:
'In the wilderness prepare the way of the Lord,
make straight in the desert a highway for our God.
Every valley shall be lifted up,
and every mountain and hill be made low;
the uneven ground shall become level,
and the rough places a plain.
Then the glory of the Lord shall be revealed,
and all people shall see it together,
for the mouth of the Lord has spoken.'

Reflection

These words of Isaiah are as relevant today as they were at their moment of expression. Today they touch our hearts as we attempt to respond to the needs of some of the most vulnerable members of society, the elderly who live alone.

Residents of care or nursing homes may also feel vulnerable in the place where they should feel safe; often they feel that they have no voice in our society today. This is a cause of shame for us as these good people have devoted their lives to the care and support of their families and communities. Now they may feel too vulnerable to ask that their most basic needs are met in a compassionate and courteous manner. They cry out to God for their pastoral and spiritual needs to receive his gracious touch at this most sacred time. This can only happen through our hands and the movements of our hearts.

Through the power of God's Holy Spirit, we recognise that the path that family carers walk is not an easy one. So often they feel isolated and alone. A recession-strapped economy has cut essential respite and other services, and exhaustion is the cross borne by these carers. In their anguish, they implore God to hear their cry as they feel so alone and do not know where to turn. Into this abyss, the Lord wishes to bring healing light and comfort.

Prayer

May I respond to the cry of all who suffer, in a way that reflects the light that you bring, O God. May I be an agent of your healing to all whom I serve in a ministry of love.
Amen.

Saturday

The home of Nazareth

Reading

Numbers 14:19

Forgive the iniquity of this people according to the greatness of your steadfast love, just as you have pardoned this people, from Egypt even until now.

Reflection

On this day we ask God to reach down to rescue all victims of domestic violence. National statistics reveal an ever-increasing rise in this form of abuse. This horrific crime robs families of peace, tranquillity and at times even the gift of human life. Men, women and children live in fear for their lives and society is shattered at its core.

Much suffering is inflicted upon innocent people in the place where they should feel comfortable, 'at home', at peace. Pain is carried deep in the human heart and a blanket of shame and guilt often prevents silent victims from seeking the help and support that they need.

Yet for those who do seek help, the root causes of this 'dis-ease' may not be addressed, and victims who have sought refuge in shelters may return home without the support that they need. Problems recur and the vicious cycle continues. All too often, a pattern of abuse continues from generation to generation as children who have witnessed violence as a response to a problem respond in the same manner in their adult lives. Fortunately, through the grace of God, good social support and education, this death-dealing pattern can be broken.

Prayer

In your coming, Lord, you desire that all homes are modelled on the home in Nazareth to be places where all may grow in the knowledge and love of God. We pray, Lord, that you touch and heal the violence that lurks in all our hearts and that only your saving grace can redeem. May our homes and our hearts be shrouded in your gentleness so that our homes may be places of gentleness, justice and peace where you, O God, may reign forever and ever.
Amen.

Questions for reflection

- What is the gift that you desire from the Lord this Advent/Christmastide?
- Why are you seeking this gift?
- If you were to receive it, how would you use it for the glory of God?

Fourth Sunday of Advent

Discerning the voice of God

Reading

Luke 1:26-38

In the sixth month the angel Gabriel was sent by God to a town in Galilee called Nazareth, to a virgin engaged to a man whose name was Joseph, of the house of David. The virgin's name was Mary. And he came to her and said, 'Greetings, favoured one! The Lord is with you.' But she was much perplexed by his words and pondered what sort of greeting this might be. The angel said to her, 'Do not be afraid, Mary, for you have found favour with God. And now, you will conceive in your womb and bear a son, and you will name him Jesus. He will be great, and will be called the Son of the Most High, and the Lord God will give to him the throne of his ancestor David. He will reign over the house of Jacob for ever, and of his kingdom there will be no end.' Mary said to the angel, 'How can this be, since I am a virgin?' The angel said to her, 'The Holy Spirit will come upon you, and the power of the Most High will overshadow you; therefore the child to be born will be holy; he will be called Son of God. And now, your relative Elizabeth in her old age has also conceived a son; and this is the sixth month for her who was said to be barren. For nothing will be impossible with God.' Then Mary said, 'Here am I, the servant of the Lord; let it be with me according to your word.' Then the angel departed from her.

Reflection

In this Gospel reading we are offered a glimpse of the inner life of Mary. She lived her life according to the word of God and found favour with him. His word was her delight and the joy of her heart. An attitude of prayerful openness and receptivity helped her to discern the voice of God even when its message was shrouded in mystery: 'How can this be, since I am a virgin?' Her humanity allowed her to be perplexed but her faith was deeper than her doubt. She waited and listened for a deeper understanding of what was being asked of her and how it might be accomplished. True to the nature of God, a life-giving way was revealed: 'The Holy Spirit will come upon you, and the power of the Most High will overshadow you.' In this action the fullness of the power of God would be revealed, and 'therefore the child to be born will be holy; he will be called Son of God.'

The mystery of what was being offered to Mary was at its most profound, but she did not shy away from the invitation and responsibility of young, single motherhood. This generous, selfless attitude must have been the fruit of a lifetime of prayerful surrender to the voice of the God who calls us. She was responding on God's terms to God's invitation, 'Here am I, the servant of the Lord; let it be with me according to your word.' In so doing she has offered us a profound example of how we, too, are invited to listen for the deep, still voice of God in our lives. We are reassured of the presence and power of the Holy Spirit with us to listen and respond to the calls of God in our lives.

Prayer

Through the power of your Holy Spirit, may I, too, be a life bearer for our world. I know, O Lord, that your promise of hope is greatly needed in the world today. May I bring good news to all the towns and valleys where you have asked me to serve you. May I share the good news that there will indeed be a light shining out of darkness in our world when our God comes amongst us (2 Corinthians 4:6).

Amen.

Monday

Create in me a pure heart

Reading

1 Thessalonians 5:23, 24

May the God of peace himself sanctify you entirely; and may your spirit and soul and body be kept sound and blameless at the coming of our Lord Jesus Christ. The one who calls you is faithful, and he will do this.

Reflection

At this most holy time of Advent, we ponder again our call to draw ever closer to the God who is to come. We are invited into a purity of relationship with God and each other that will help to prepare our hearts for the coming of the King of heaven and earth. By the power and grace of the Holy Spirit we will be able to live the kinds of lives that the Lord wants us to live.

'So we have known and believe the love that God has for us. God is love, and those who abide in love abide in God, and God abides in them' (1 John 4:16). Every area of our lives and every part of the world has to surrender to the one who is to come if peace is to reign and our God is to be made welcome among us.

As frail human beings we are ever mindful of our tendency to wander far from God's precepts. We are reminded that 'I am of the flesh, sold into slavery under sin. I do not understand my own actions. For I do not do what I want, but I do the very thing I hate . . . But in fact it is no longer I that do it, but sin that dwells within me' (Romans 7:14-17). But in love he keeps calling us back to him. We know who it is who has rescued us and we are grateful: 'Who will rescue me from this body of death? Thanks be to God through Jesus Christ our Lord!' (Romans 7:24, 25). This desire to remain faithful and draw closer to God is a fruit of the Holy Spirit at work in our lives. It is his free gift to us, and he desires that we seek his grace to deepen our relationship with him at this time of Advent. We are invited to indeed 'prepare the way of the Lord, make his paths straight' in our hearts (Mark 1:3). In all that we do he asks us to 'do everything for the glory of God' (1 Corinthians 10:31). In so doing, God himself will sanctify us entirely (1 Thessalonians 5:23, 24). Our Advent will truly be a celebration of God's goodness to us, as 'the free gift of God is eternal life in Christ Jesus our Lord' (Romans 6:23).

Prayer

Lord, may your coming cleanse my heart of all sin. May I desire to draw closer to you every moment of my life. May the fullness of your presence within my soul grow and deepen each day. May I share your joy with all your people, O God.
Amen.

Tuesday

Obedience

Reading

Matthew 1:18-25

Now the birth of Jesus the Messiah took place in this way. When his mother Mary had been engaged to Joseph, but before they lived together, she was found to be with child from the Holy Spirit. Her husband Joseph, being a righteous man and unwilling to expose her to public disgrace, planned to dismiss her quietly. But just when he had resolved to do this, an angel of the Lord appeared to him in a dream and said, 'Joseph, son of David, do not be afraid to take Mary as your wife, for the child conceived in her is from the Holy Spirit. She will bear a son, and you are to name him Jesus, for he will save his people from their sins. All this took place to fulfil what had been spoken by the Lord through the prophet:

> 'Look, the virgin shall conceive and bear a son,
> and they shall name him Emmanuel',

which means, 'God is with us.' When Joseph awoke from sleep, he did as the angel of the Lord commanded him; he took her as his wife, but had no marital relations with her until she had borne a son; and he named him Jesus.

Reflection

Once again we learn of the intervention of God in the world. Mary has found favour with God in a way that had never been known before. The conception of the child within her was an act of compassionate grace for the redemption of all. It was surrounded in mystery.

Mary's fiancé, Joseph, a man of honour, was at a loss to understand what was happening to them. His prayer echoed the prayer of Paul when he asked, 'who has known the mind of the Lord?' (1 Corinthians 2:16). He prayed and, following the intervention of the angel to him in a dream, echoed the response of Abraham of old:

> No distrust made him waver concerning the promise of God, but he grew strong in his faith as he gave glory to God, being fully convinced that God was able to do what he had promised.
>
> *Romans 4:20, 21*

Joseph obeyed and took Mary home as his wife. In this environment of faithful love and unreserved, obedient listening, Emmanuel was born to us. The listening, faithful and obedient trust of Mary and Joseph allowed the one who was to free the people from their sins to come amongst us. Our prayer and faithful listening to the voice of the Holy Spirit in our lives can enable us, too, to be partakers in this redemptive mission in our world today.

Prayer

I offer praise and eternal thanks for a virgin girl and a wood-carving gentleman. They brought forth the life and love of the eternal God who has rescued me from my sin. May my life worship and honour him who is redemptive love through my acts of obedient listening. Amen.

Wednesday

God blesses his people

Reading

Luke 1:5-25

In the days of King Herod of Judea, there was a priest named Zechariah, who belonged to the priestly order of Abijah. His wife was a descendant of Aaron, and her name was Elizabeth. Both of them were righteous before God, living blamelessly according to all the commandments and regulations of the Lord. But they had no children, because Elizabeth was barren, and both were getting on in years.

Once when he was serving as priest before God and his section was on duty, he was chosen by lot, according to the custom of the priesthood, to enter the sanctuary of the Lord and offer incense. Now at the time of the incense-offering, the whole assembly of the people was praying outside. Then there appeared to him an angel of the Lord, standing at the right side of the altar of incense. When Zechariah saw him, he was terrified; and fear overwhelmed him. But the angel said to him, 'Do not be afraid, Zechariah, for your prayer has been heard. Your wife Elizabeth will bear you a son, and you will name him John. You will have joy and gladness, and many will rejoice at his birth, for he will be great in the sight of the Lord. He must never drink wine or strong drink; even before his birth he will be filled with the Holy Spirit. He will turn many of the people of Israel to the Lord their God. With the spirit and power of Elijah he will go before him, to turn the hearts of parents to their children, and the disobedient to the wisdom of the righteous, to make ready a people prepared for the Lord.' Zechariah said to the angel, 'How will I know that this is so? For I am an old man, and my wife is getting on in years.' The angel replied, 'I am Gabriel. I stand in the presence of God, and I have been sent to speak to you and to bring you this good news. But now, because you did not believe my words, which will be fulfilled in their time, you will become mute, unable to speak, until the days these things occur.'

Meanwhile, the people were waiting for Zechariah, and wondered at his delay in the sanctuary. When he did come out, he could not speak to them, and they realised that he had seen a vision in the sanctuary. He kept motioning to them and remained unable to speak. When his time of service was ended, he went to his home.

After those days his wife Elizabeth conceived, and for five months she remained in seclusion. She said, 'This is what the Lord has done for me when he looked favourably on me and took away the disgrace I have endured among my people.'

Reflection

In this reading we learn once more of the faithfulness of God to all people of goodwill. He visits his people who keep his laws as holy and bestows great blessings upon them. Zechariah was going about God's business in the sanctuary of the Lord and God reached into his vulnerability in a way never known before.

Zechariah was an old man who had taken the words of God into the inner recesses of his soul and lived by them. The manna of his soul were the words, 'You shall love the Lord your God with all your heart, and with all your soul, and with all your might' (Deuteronomy 6:5). These words became his food for his journey, and in him and his wife Elizabeth God saw an image of himself. 'Then God said, "Let us make humankind in our image, according to our likeness"' (Genesis 1:26). He looked with love on Zechariah and his wife Elizabeth and sent an angel of good news to them. This angel bore healing in its wings for Zechariah and Elizabeth, and also for the human race in the person of the child they were to bear.

Encounters with angels are an unusual phenomenon. We can empathise with Zechariah in his moment of dread. The angel identified himself as Gabriel. He reached into the fear of Zechariah and explained the new mission of parenthood that awaited a couple who had longed for a child but who had passed their reproductive prime. The ethical challenges of human reproductive science that challenge our world today had not yet been conceived.

Infused with the Holy Spirit from this moment forward, the child would bear healing, joy and gladness for all. He would live a holy and blameless life consecrated to the Lord. He would clearly outline the rules and norms of a God-centred life. His followers would be expected to live a covenant relationship with God and worship him night and day.

This message was too incomprehensible for a man of prayer whose faith was shaken by a visit from the supernatural. I can empathise with Zechariah because I, too, have been overwhelmed and awestruck at the marvels of God. Gabriel reached down to Zechariah and promised him that the words which he spoke would 'be fulfilled in their time'; God's timing is always perfect. Zechariah continued with his task of offering incense to the Lord and later returned to the 'outside world'. Immediately, the people recognised that something mysterious had taken place and Zechariah returned home to his wife Elizabeth.

God showered the blessing of pregnancy upon them and Elizabeth withdrew to give praise to the God who reached down and rescued her from all her distress.

In you, O Lord, I take refuge;
let me never be put to shame.
In your righteousness deliver me and rescue me;
incline your ear to me and save me.
Be to me a rock of refuge,
a strong fortress, to save me,
for you are my rock and my fortress.

Psalm 71:1-3

She pondered on the mystery and beauty of God. Their souls rejoiced as they awaited the birth of the miracle child foretold by an angel of God.

Prayer

May my heart, too, be surprised by joy during this holy season of Advent. May the fear which blocks my faith be removed by a new infusion of the Holy Spirit. May I desire to live a covenant relationship with the God who is to come. May I pray in new ways for all who are struggling with the heartache of barrenness. May your healing touch bestow upon your chosen ones the gift of a child. May all involved in reproductive science be guided by the light of your Holy Spirit. May all parents proclaim, 'Look what the Lord has done for us; indeed we are glad.'
Amen.

Thursday

The benevolence of God

Reading

Luke 1:26-38

In the sixth month the angel Gabriel was sent by God to a town in Galilee called Nazareth, to a virgin engaged to a man whose name was Joseph, of the house of David. The virgin's name was Mary. And he came to her and said, 'Greetings, favoured one! The Lord is with you.' But she was much perplexed by his words and pondered what sort of greeting this might be. The angel said to her, 'Do not be afraid, Mary, for you have found favour with God. And now, you will conceive in your womb and bear a son, and you will name him Jesus. He will be great, and will be called the Son of the Most High, and the Lord God will give to him the throne of his ancestor David. He will reign over the house of Jacob for ever, and of his kingdom there will be no end.' Mary said to the angel, 'How can this be, since I am a virgin?' The angel said to her, 'The Holy Spirit will come upon you, and the power of the Most High will overshadow you; therefore the child to be born will be holy; he will be called Son of God. And now, your relative Elizabeth in her old age has also conceived a son; and this is the sixth month for her who was said to be barren. For nothing will be impossible with God.' Then Mary said, 'Here am I, the servant of the Lord; let it be with me according to your word.' Then the angel departed from her.

Reflection

In this Gospel reading we learn of the intimacy of God with his people in a new way. He desires to become human and to live amongst us. This will only be possible if a woman accepts an invitation to bear his Son. God chooses a woman who has shown her desire and capacity for commitment; she is engaged to a man named Joseph. An obedient angel goes on a mission to this young woman to reveal to her what God's plans for her are.

'Greetings, favoured one! The Lord is with you.' His greeting is warm and reveals to Mary the intimacy that God shares with her. She is a favoured daughter of the Lord. God wishes to share his divine nature with her in the person of a child, whom she will bear and carry to birth. She is naturally perturbed as she has not yet consummated her relationship with Joseph. The angel promises her that the intimacy of God through the power of the Holy Spirit will bring this life-changing event to fruition. Conceived of God, the child will be holy.

The benevolence of God has also been bestowed on an older lady, Elizabeth. The tears of barrenness have given way to the joy of motherhood. The intimacy shared by expectant mothers is gifted on Mary. Her self-surrender is revealed in her desire to partake in this wonderful mystery: 'Here am I, the servant of the Lord; let it be with me according to your word.' The mission of the angel of light is complete and he departs from her.

During this Advent season we, too, are invited to share a deepening intimacy with God. We are the favoured people of the Lord. Jesus will be born again in our hearts and lives if we are open to the power and grace of God's Holy Spirit. Our lives, like Mary's, will be transformed. We are invited and challenged to allow our faith to grow deeper. The intimacy of union with God is being bestowed upon us in ever new ways. We are invited to ask for the grace of the Holy Spirit so that we may recognise God's calls to us in our everyday lives. 'Angels' come to us in different ways, if only we can recognise them. We pray that we may have the grace to respond as Mary did. The mission that God is asking of us will be revealed when we sincerely offer the following prayer.

Prayer

'Here am I, the servant of the Lord; let it be with me according to your word.' My heart will echo the prayer of the angel – 'nothing will be impossible with God.' The tears of my own particular barrenness will give way to the joy of a new and deeper life in God. I rejoice and am glad.
Amen.

Friday

The pilgrimage of pregnancy

Reading

Luke 1:39-45

In those days Mary set out and went with haste to a Judean town in the hill country, where she entered the house of Zechariah and greeted Elizabeth. When Elizabeth heard Mary's greeting, the child leapt in her womb. And Elizabeth was filled with the Holy Spirit and exclaimed with a loud cry, 'Blessed are you among women, and blessed is the fruit of your womb. And why has this happened to me, that the mother of my Lord comes to me? For as soon as I heard the sound of your greeting, the child in my womb leapt for joy. And blessed is she who believed that there would be a fulfilment of what was spoken to her by the Lord.'

Reflection

In this lovely reading we learn of the response of Mary to the message of the angel. She did not delay and 'went with haste' to share the pilgrimage of pregnancy with Elizabeth. There is no mention of anyone accompanying Mary through the hill country to the Judean town. She trusts in her mission of ministry to an older woman who is with child. Her desire to support another is her primary concern. Her generosity is acknowledged in the prayer of Elizabeth – 'the mother of my Lord comes to me' – she who is to bear a blessed child. The child, too, leaps in joy. The faith and unyielding trust of Mary is acknowledged.

We are offered a wonderful example of generous self-gift in the life and mission of Mary. Concern for another was rooted in the kernel of her soul. The mutual ministry of woman to woman during their time of unbounded fruitfulness is blessed. Elizabeth declares with great joy that the child to be born to Mary is holy. This may not have been revealed at this time if Mary had not generously reached out to Elizabeth, but she did. Their joy was full.

In our own lives, God invites us to reach out in love to the needs of others. We are participants in the great mystery of redemption and salvation as we are the favoured ones. Our God is coming to us in new ways this Advent.

Prayer

May I recognise you, O God, when I reach out to all in need. May my life be holy and blessed and may I draw ever closer to you. May my trust in his mission of love and the faith of my soul deepen. In due course, may my own joy be full.
Amen.

Saturday

Consumed with delight

Reading

Luke 1:46-55

And Mary said,
'My soul magnifies the Lord,
and my spirit rejoices in God my Saviour,
for he has looked with favour on the lowliness of his servant.
Surely, from now on all generations will call me blessed;
for the Mighty One has done great things for me,
and holy is his name.
His mercy is for those who fear him
from generation to generation.
He has shown strength with his arm;
he has scattered the proud in the thoughts of their hearts.
He has brought down the powerful from their thrones,
and lifted up the lowly;
he has filled the hungry with good things,
and sent the rich away empty.
He has helped his servant Israel,
in remembrance of his mercy,
according to the promise he made to our ancestors,
to Abraham and to his descendants for ever.'
And Mary remained with her for about three months
and then returned to her home.

Reflection

Mary sings this beautiful song of praise to the 'Mighty One' who has visited her in her nothingness and blessed her life in the most wonderful way. She humbly acknowledges that she is the favoured of the Lord and she rejoices. Consumed with delight, she speaks of the richness of the relationship that she shares with her 'Saviour'.

Mary blesses God and encourages all to share in her fidelity of relationship with the God who saves. She offers all of God's people a code of living that will enable them to have a life-giving, faith-filled relationship with God. She reassures us that God is merciful and also reminds us that he expects us all to live in a new way. Holiness of life will be bestowed on all who live by God's truth, as it was bestowed on Mary.

Prayer

During this Advent season, I am gifted with another opportunity to draw closer to the Son of God. I will learn a new way of living from him. In his mercy he will draw me closer to his Father and to all humankind. I will be blessed by the Lord and my joy will increase. This will indeed be a wonderful Advent gift. I rejoice and give thanks.
Amen.

Questions for reflection

- Do I rejoice in God's goodness to me?
- If not, what blocks my sense of gratitude and rejoicing?
- What attitudes do I have that need to change so that I may rejoice more fully?
- Am I open to the graces of this wonderful season of Advent so that I may be filled with a spirit of gratitude and rejoicing?

23rd December

God is faithful

Reading

Luke 1:57-66

Now the time came for Elizabeth to give birth, and she bore a son. Her neighbours and relatives heard that the Lord had shown his great mercy to her, and they rejoiced with her.

On the eight day they came to circumcise the child, and they were going to name him Zechariah after his father. But his mother said, 'No; he is to be called John.' They said to her, 'None of your relatives has this name.' Then they began motioning to his father to find out what name he wanted to give him. He asked for a writing-tablet and wrote, 'His name is John.' And all of them were amazed. Immediately his mouth was opened and his tongue freed, and he began to speak, praising God. Fear came over all their neighbours, and all these things were talked about throughout the entire hill country of Judea.

Reflection

The power and mystery of God consume us as we await with expectant hearts the unfolding of the promises of God. Advent is drawing to a close and our longing for the one who is to come increases. A new dawn is on the horizon and our hearts are full of joy. We enter into the joy and expectancy of Elizabeth as she prepared to give birth to her child. She had never expected that her life would bear a child, but now her time had come. We are filled with awe and wonder at the graciousness of God. We share in the joy of her neighbours and friends and we listen to the lesson that is gifted to us through his birth.

Like Mary, Elizabeth had listened intently to the voice of God and wished to obey. She overrode tradition in the choice of name for her child and asked that he be called John. Zechariah lost his speech in the temple when he questioned God. He now wrote the name of their child for all to see. His doubt was washed away by the mercy of God, and in this act of obedience his speech was restored. A hymn of praise was offered to God by all who witnessed this great event. People were challenged to think more deeply about the intervention of God in their lives and to give him thanks. They believed that a mysterious mission awaited the child but had to wait patiently as it unfolded.

Our lives are touched by this event, too. We are reminded of our need to trust God and not to doubt. We are asked to listen intently to the voice of God and to obey the message that is offered to us. We are to be unafraid to stand for truth and to break with tradition if necessary. We are to be open to allowing the light of God to shine forth no matter what the cost. Often, we will be surprised by the gifts and challenges that await us as we listen and obey the still, small voice of the Spirit of God. In faith, we will learn that God is faithful to his promises and does not disappoint. Like Elizabeth and Zechariah, our hearts will rejoice. We will have opportunities to bear witness to the power and the glory of the living God.

Prayer

During this Advent time, may my faith in the living God grow deeper. Like Elizabeth, may I believe that God is

faithful to his promises and that his plans for my life are good. May no fear block my desire to walk in his ways and to serve him with my whole life. In trust, I make this prayer to the living God.
Amen.

Christmas Eve

A call to holiness

Reading

Luke 1:67-79

Then his father Zechariah was filled with the Holy Spirit and spoke this prophecy:
'Blessed be the Lord God of Israel,
for he has looked favourably on his people and redeemed them.
He has raised up a mighty saviour for us
in the house of his servant David,
as he spoke through the mouth of his holy prophets from of old,
that we would be saved from our enemies and from the hand of all who hate us.
Thus he has shown the mercy promised to our ancestors,
and has remembered his holy covenant,
the oath that he swore to our ancestor Abraham,
to grant us that we, being rescued from the hands of our enemies,
might serve him without fear, in holiness and righteousness
before him all our days.
And you, child, will be called the prophet of the Most High;
for you will go before the Lord to prepare his ways,
to give knowledge of salvation to his people
by the forgiveness of their sins.
By the tender mercy of our God,
the dawn from on high will break upon us,
to give light to those who sit in darkness and in the

shadow of death,
to guide our feet into the way of peace.'

Reflection

This is a hymn of thanksgiving which we are invited to share. The prophecies of old have been honoured. God has looked with mercy and love on all humankind and rescued us from all evil. He has sent us his Son. Our hearts rejoice.

In his birth we hear a call to a life of deep holiness. We are asked to serve all of God's people and live according to God's law. We are the chosen people of God who are guided by the eternal one who dwells amongst us. The Prince of Peace has come amongst us and will guide our world in his way of peace if we cooperate with his will for the world. We know that peace is the fruit of justice and we desire to live by his law of love. Like Simeon, we, too, will be able to sing our own hymn of praise to the God who has chosen to live amongst us (Luke 2:25-35). We rejoice and give thanks.

Prayer

I prepare my heart for your birth. I give you thanks for coming to live among us. You bless me with your presence and call me into a deeper life with you. I pray for all who are far from home at this time. May the bonds of the human family be enriched by your birth. May the world know your peace, a peace the world cannot give.
I make all this prayer in your name, O gracious God, God of all goodness.
Amen.

Christmas Day

Magnificat

(author's own composition as a point of reflection)

Mary attended to the word of God;
glorified 'The Word',
nurtured the Lamb of God.
Ever fruitful in fidelity,
she invoked the Holy Spirit on humanity.
Invited all into union with 'The One'
she bore and carried to birth,
cared for with human hands,
listened to with human ears
and the inner ear of her heart.

Mary attended to the needs of the poor,
at all times and in all places,
where she was led by the inner voice of love.

Mary adored eternally 'The Word'
who is all wisdom,
offering,
redeeming,
divine Son of God.

An invitation

You may wish to reflect on the gifts that God has bestowed upon you this year.

Savour for a moment the gifts that have been bestowed upon you by family, friends and community.

In what ways have your faith and prayer been enriched by your celebration of Advent and Christmas?

What differences might these gifts make to your own life, the life of your family/community and the global community?

Write a prayer or letter of thanks to God for all who have supported you on your journey of faith.